Clouds

by Erin Edison

Consulting Editor: Gail Saunders-Smith, PhD

CAPSTONE PRESS
a capstone imprint

Pebble Plus is published by Capstone Press,
1710 Roe Crest Drive, North Mankato, Minnesota 56003.
www.capstonepub.com

Copyright © 2012 by Capstone Press, a Capstone imprint. All rights reserved.
No part of this publication may be reproduced in whole or in part, or stored in a retrieval system, or transmitted in any form or by any means, electronic, mechanical, photocopying, recording, or otherwise, without written permission of the publisher. For information regarding permission, write to Capstone Press,
1710 Roe Crest Drive, North Mankato, Minnesota 56003.

Library of Congress Cataloging-in-Publication Data
Edison, Erin.
  Clouds / by Erin Edison.
    p. cm.—(Pebble plus. Weather basics)
  Summary: "Simple text and full-color photographs describe how clouds form and the different types of clouds"—Provided by publisher.
  Includes bibliographical references and index.
  ISBN 978-1-4296-6057-0 (library binding)
  ISBN 978-1-4296-7077-7 (paperback)
  ISBN 978-1-4296-8751-5 (saddle-stitch)
  1. Clouds—Juvenile literature. 2. Clouds—Diurnal variations—Juvenile literature. I. Title. II. Series.
  QC921.35.E35 2012
  551.57'6—dc22   2010053936

Editorial Credits
Erika L. Shores, editor; Kyle Grenz, designer; Laura Manthe, production specialist

Photo Credits
Dreamstime: Robert Adrian Hillman, 11; Getty Images Inc.: The Image Bank/Tyler Stableford, 21; Shutterstock: 2happy, back cover, andreiuc88, 19, Christophe Testi, 17, Dudarev Mikhail, 9, Gulei Ivan, cover, Nataliia Melnychuk, 5, TobagoCays, 15, tonobalaguerf, 13, vovan, 1, Yuriy Kulyk, 7

Artistic Effects
Shutterstock: marcus55

Capstone Press thanks Mike Shores, earth science teacher at RBA Public Charter School in Mankato, Minnesota, for his assistance on this book.

Note to Parents and Teachers

The Weather Basics series supports national science standards related to earth science. This book describes and illustrates clouds. The images support early readers in understanding the text. The repetition of words and phrases helps early readers learn new words. This book also introduces early readers to subject-specific vocabulary words, which are defined in the Glossary section. Early readers may need assistance to read some words and to use the Table of Contents, Glossary, Read More, Internet Sites, and Index sections of the book.

Table of Contents

What Are Clouds?..... 4
Types of Clouds 10
Wind Moves Clouds ...20

Glossary.....................22
Read More 23
Internet Sites.............23
Index..........................24

What Are Clouds?

Clouds move across the sky.

Clouds can be all shapes and sizes.

Some clouds are big and puffy.

Others are thin and wispy.

Clouds form when warm air rises and cools. Tiny water droplets stick to dust and other particles in the air to make clouds.

Clouds drop precipitation on land. Snow falls when the air is 32 degrees Fahrenheit (0 degrees Celsius) or lower. Rain falls when it's warmer.

Types of Clouds

Scientists study cloud shapes. The shapes tell what kind of weather is coming. Cirrus clouds are high and thin. They mean good weather.

Cumulus clouds have flat bottoms and puffy tops. Small, white cumulus clouds mean we'll have good weather.

Cumulonimbus clouds mean bad weather is coming. These tall, puffy clouds bring thunderstorms, hail, and even tornadoes.

Gray, flat stratus clouds cover most of the sky. They form low in the sky. Snow or rain sometimes falls from stratus clouds.

Fog is a cloud too. Fog happens when a cloud forms near the ground. Fog goes away when wind and heat evaporate the water.

Wind Moves Clouds

Clouds carry rain and snow. Wind pushes clouds across the sky. Clouds bring water to places all over the world.

Glossary

droplet—a small drop of liquid

evaporate—the action of a liquid changing into a gas; heat causes water to evaporate

hail—balls of ice that form in clouds and fall to the ground

particle—a tiny piece of something; water droplets stick to dust, salt, and other tiny particles in the air to form clouds

precipitation—water that falls from clouds to the earth's surface; precipitation can be rain, hail, sleet, or snow

tornado—a large, twisting cloud that produces high winds; tornadoes form over land

Read More

Flanagan, Alice K. *Rain.* Weather Watch. Mankato, Minn.: Child's World, Inc., 2010.

Goldsmith, Mike. *The Weather.* Now We Know About. New York: Crabtree Pub., 2010.

Sterling, Kristin. *It's Cloudy Today.* What's the Weather Like? Minneapolis: Lerner Publications Co., 2010.

Internet Sites

FactHound offers a safe, fun way to find Internet sites related to this book. All of the sites on FactHound have been researched by our staff.

Here's all you do:

Visit www.facthound.com

Type in this code: 9781429660570

Check out projects, games and lots more at www.capstonekids.com

Index

cirrus clouds, 10
cumulonimbus clouds, 14
cumulus clouds, 12
evaporation, 18
fog, 18
hail, 14
particles, 6
precipitation, 8, 14, 16 20

rain, 8, 16, 20
snow, 8, 16, 20
stratus clouds, 16
thunderstorms, 14
tornadoes, 14
water droplets, 6
wind, 18, 20

Word Count: 194
Grade: 1
Early-Intervention Level: 19